Feelings

I'M Tired

and other body feelings

Clare Hibbert

Illustrated by Simona Dimitri

Evans

Published by Evans Brothers Limited
2A Portman Mansions, Chiltern Street, London W1U 6NR

© Evans Brothers Limited 2010
Concept devised for Evans Brothers by Clare Hibbert

Editor: Clare Hibbert
Designer: Sandra Perry
Picture researcher: Sophie Schrey
Illustrator: Simona Dimitri (Milan Illustration Agency)
Sign language artist: Rob Perry

British Library Cataloguing in Publication Data
Hibbert, Clare, 1970-
Tired!. -- (Feelings)
1. Fatigue--Juvenile literature.
I. Title II. Series
152.1'886-dc22

ISBN-13: 9780237542009

Printed & bound in China by New Era Printing Co. Ltd.

**The signing instructions in this book follow British Sign Language.
The visual instructions show a mirror image to make it easier for
you to practise your own signing in front of a mirror.**

CONTENTS

Tired

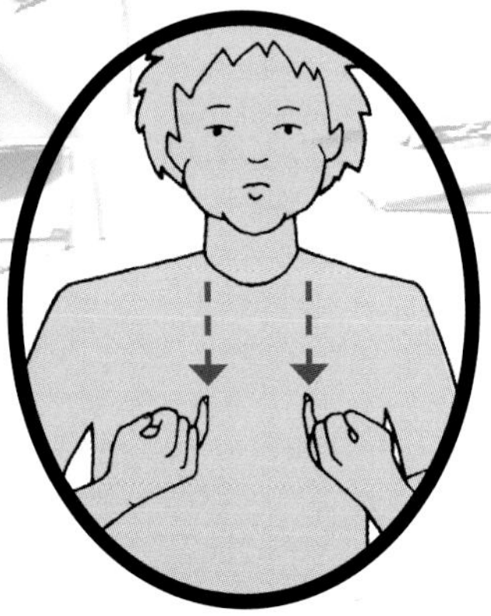

s-t-r-e-t-c-h

yawn

4

tired

hungry

thirsty

full up

It's been an exciting day. But now I feel **tired**.

Night, night!

sick

dizzy

cold

poorly

sore

Hungry

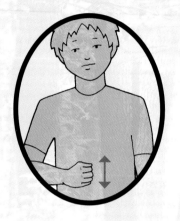

We went on a long walk. Then I felt **hungry**.

rumble, rumble

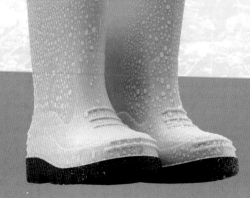

6

tired

hungry

thirsty

full up

OK. Let's go and have lunch!

sniff

sick   dizzy   cold   poorly   sore

Thirsty

8

tired

hungry

thirsty

full up

I imagined living in a desert. I felt **thirsty**!

Jingle, jangle

sick

dizzy

cold

poorly

sore

Full up

chatter, chatter

click

tired

hungry

thirsty

full up

10

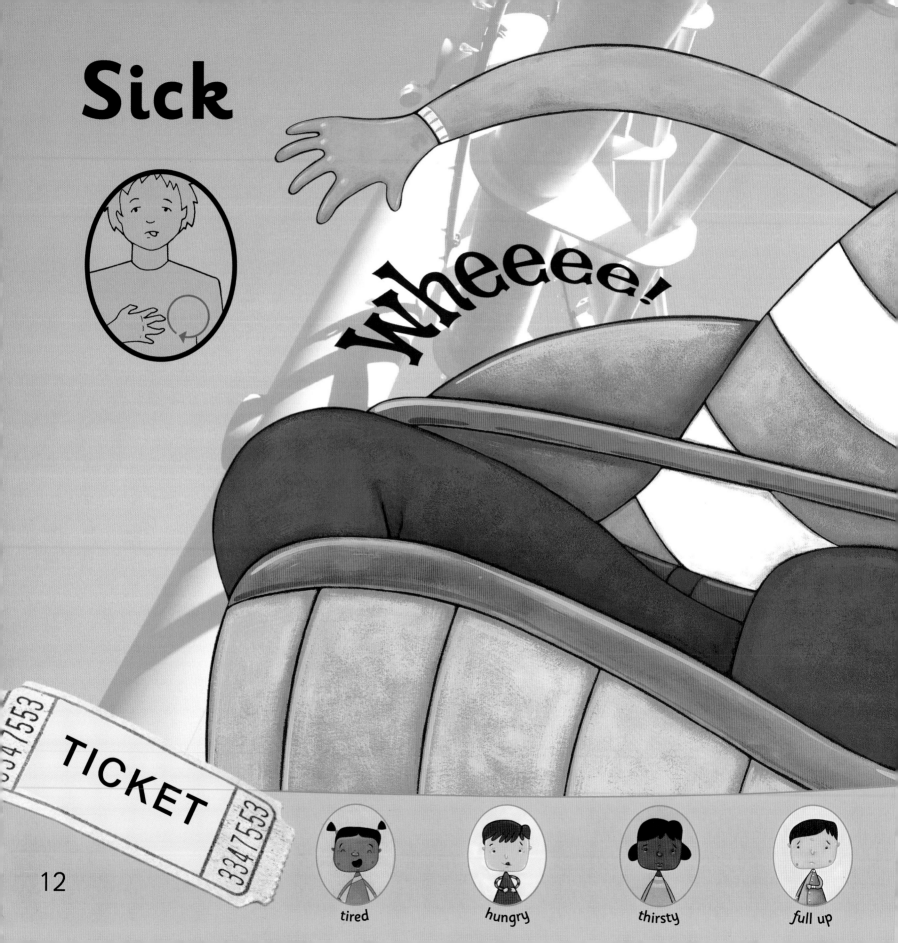

Sick

Wheeee!

TICKET

3347553

12

tired | hungry | thirsty | full up

I went on the scary ride at the fair. I felt **sick**!

zoom!

sick   dizzy   cold   poorly   sore

Dizzy

Whooosh!

tired

hungry

thirsty

full up

Cold

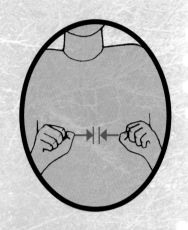

I dreamed I was playing snowballs. I felt **cold**.

shiver shiver

tired

hungry

thirsty

full up

brrr!

sick

dizzy

cold

poorly

sore

17

Poorly

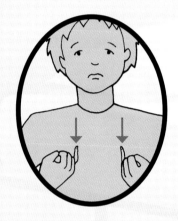

brrmm, brrmm

tired

hungry

thirsty

full up

18

19

Sore

I woke up after my operation. My throat felt **sore**.

Croak, croak!

tired   hungry   thirsty   full up

Notes for adults

The **Feelings** series has been designed to support and extend the learning of young children. The books link in to the Early Years curriculum and beyond. Find out more about Early Years and reading with children from the National Literacy Trust (www.literacytrust.org.uk).

The **Feelings** series helps to develop children's knowledge, understanding and skills in key social and emotional aspects of learning (SEAL), in particular empathy, self-awareness and social skills. It aims to help children understand, articulate and manage their feelings. Visit http://nationalstrategies.standards.dcsf.gov.uk/node/87009 to find out more about SEAL.

Titles in the series:

I'm Happy and other fun feelings looks at positive emotions
I'm Sad and other tricky feelings looks at uncomfortable emotions
I'm Tired and other body feelings looks at physical feelings
I'm Busy a feelings story explores other familiar feelings

The **Feelings** books offer the following special features:

1) **matching game**
   a border of faces gives readers the chance to hunt out the face that matches the sensation covered on the spread;
2) **signing instructions**
   each spread includes clear visual instructions for signing the emotion (these follow British Sign Language standard – visit britishsignlanguage.com for more information about this organisation);
3) **fantasy scenes**
   since children often explore emotion through stories, dreams and their imaginations, two emotions (in this book, 'thirsty' and 'cold') are presented in a fantasy setting, giving the opportunity to examine intense feelings in the safety of an unreal context.

Making the most of reading time

When reading with younger children, take time to explore the pictures together. Ask children to find, identify, count or describe different objects. Point out colours and textures. Pause in your reading so that children can ask questions, repeat your words or even predict the next word. This sort of participation develops early reading skills.

Follow the words with your finger as you read. The main text is in Infant Sassoon, a clear, friendly font designed for children learning to read and write. The thought and speech bubbles and sound effects add fun and give the opportunity to distinguish between levels of communication.

Extend children's learning by using this book as a springboard for discussion and follow-on activities. Here are a few ideas:

Pages 4–5: I feel tired

Do the children know the story of the 'Princess and the Pea'? Provide old magazines so that each child can make her a patterned 'mattress', then assemble a super-tall mural of the princess's bed. Don't forget to put in the pea and the princess! You could also find pictures of different kinds of bed, such as a Moses' basket, cot, bunk beds, hammock, four-poster and futon, then see how many the children can name. Use Internet or museum resources to find images of beds used long ago.

Pages 6–7: I feel hungry

Encourage children to keep a pictorial food diary for a week. The children can draw what they eat for breakfast, lunch, dinner and snack times each day. Older children might enjoy being given blank clock faces to stick into their diaries – they can add clock hands to record what time they ate each meal.

Pages 8–9: I feel thirsty

Help the children to make thirst-quenching fruity cocktails. Allow them to carefully pour some apple juice into the bottom of a tall plastic beaker, add slices of fresh fruit and then top up with still water or reduced-sugar lemonade. For the finishing touch, they can add a couple of bendy straws or cocktail umbrellas (be careful – the sticks are sharp).

Pages 10–11: I feel full up

Play-act running a restaurant. Help the children design simple picture menus of the food and drinks, and practise laying tables with tablecloths, napkins and cutlery. Children can take turns being aproned restaurant staff or dressed-up diners.

Pages 12–13: I feel sick

If the children have ever visited a fun fair or theme park, ask them to think of different words that express the sensations they felt. Did they prefer fast rides or slow ones? Can they draw or paint pictures of themselves having fun at the fair? Write on sound effects, such as 'Whoosh!' and 'Wheeee!'.

Pages 14–15: I feel dizzy

Ask the children to draw a map of their local playground. Where are the swings, the roundabout and the slide? What other things are there? What do they like best?

Pages 16–17: I feel cold

Create a 'cold' collage of Arctic animals. Draw thick outlines first, then stick on screwed-up tissue-paper balls to fill in the shapes: white for polar bears, icebergs and snowflakes, grey for seals and blue for any expanses of ocean water.

Pages 18–19: I feel poorly

The brothers in this picture have chicken pox. Have the children ever had chicken pox, and can they remember how it felt? Ask them to design a get-well card for a friend who's not well.

Pages 20–21: I feel sore

Think about ways children could pass the time while recovering in hospital from an operation. Gentle activities can take their mind off feeling sore or uncomfortable. The memory game is a great quiet game. Put ten familiar objects on a tray. While the players close their eyes, take away one object. Who will be first to guess which object is missing?

23

Sign language

cold 16

dizzy 14

full up 10

hungry 6

poorly 18

sick 12

sore 20

thirsty 8

tired 4

Index

Credits

**The publisher would like to thank the following
for permission to reproduce their images:**
iStockphoto: cover and 4–5 (scorpion56), 6–7 (AVTG),
6 (slacroix), 8–9 (BremecR), 8bl (muratsen), 8c (Petershort),
8tr (enot-poloskun), 10–11 (manley099), 10 (borisyankov),
12–13 (P_Wei), 12 (davidp), 14–15 (DanBrandenburg),
14 (VMJones), 16–17 (skhoward), 16 (drnadig), 17
(zeremski), 18–19 (vicnt), 18 (carlosalvarez), 20 (belknap);
Shutterstock Images: 4 (photomak), 20–21 (wxin).